THE TELEPHONE AND TIME MANAGEMENT:
Making It a Tool and Not a Tyrant

Dru Scott, Ph.D.

A FIFTY-MINUTE™ SERIES BOOK

CRISP PUBLICATIONS, INC.
Menlo Park, California

THE TELEPHONE AND TIME MANAGEMENT:

Making It a Tool and Not a Tyrant

Dru Scott, Ph.D.

CREDITS
Editor: **Michael G. Crisp**
Designer: **Carol Harris**
Typesetting: **Interface Studio**
Cover Design: **Carol Harris**
Artwork: **Ralph Mapson**

Copyright © 1988, 1984 Dru Scott, Ph.D. (Originally published as *The Telephone: Tool or Tyrant* Signal Publishing, San Francisco).
Printed in the United States of America

English language Crisp books are distributed worldwide. Our major international distributors include:

CANADA: Reid Publishing Ltd., Box 69559—109 Thomas St., Oakville, Ontario Canada L6J 7R4. TEL: (416) 842-4428, FAX: (416) 842-9327

AUSTRALIA: Career Builders, P. O. Box 1051, Springwood, Brisbane, Queensland, Australia 4127. TEL: 841-1061, FAX: 841-1580

NEW ZEALAND: Career Builders, P. O. Box 571, Manurewa, Auckland, New Zealand. TEL: 266-5276, FAX: 266-4152

JAPAN: Phoenix Associates Co., Mizuho Bldg. 2-12-2, Kami Osaki, Shinagawa-Ku, Tokyo 141, Japan. TEL: 3-443-7231, FAX: 3-443-7640

Selected Crisp titles are also available in other languages. Contact International Rights Manager Tim Polk at (800) 442-7477 for more information.

Library of Congress Catalog Card Number 88-70489
Scott, Dru
Time Management and the Telephone
ISBN 0-931961-53-X

This book is printed on recyclable paper with soy ink.

PRINTED WITH
SOY INK

Dedicated to
the more than 100,000 people
who have participated in Dru Scott Seminars.

Thank you for your questions,
challenges, energy, and ideas.

You provided the laboratory
to test and prove the ideas in this book.

and to

Cally Curtis,
Cally Curtis Films, Hollywood

For your enthusiastic agreement
on the importance of time management
and the telephone.

You provided a great example
of how a manager leads the way
to profitable and pleasurable telephoning.

ABOUT THIS BOOK

THE TELEPHONE AND TIME MANAGEMENT is not like most books. It stands out from other self-help books in an important way. It's not a book to read—it's a book to *use*. The unique "self-paced" format of this book and the many worksheets, encourage a reader to get involved and, use some new ideas immediately.

This book will help you get more done in less time, with fewer frustrations whenever you use the telephone for business.

THE TELEPHONE AND TIME MANAGEMENT (and other books listed in the back of this book) can be used effectively in a number of ways. Here are some possibilities:

—**Individual Study.** Because the book is self-instructional, all that is needed is a quiet place, some time and a pencil. By completing the activities and exercises, a reader should receive practical ideas on how to conduct a quality job interview.

—**As a Film Guide for** *The Telephone Tool or Tyrant*, from Cally Curtis Films, Inc. (For more information about this best-selling film, contact the Cally Curtis Company, 1111 North Las Palmas Ave. Hollywood, CA 90038, (213) 467-1101.)

—**Workshops and Seminars.** The book is ideal for assigned reading *prior* to a workshop or seminar. With the basics in hand, the quality of the participation will improve, and more time can be spent on concept extensions and applications during the program. The book is also effective when it is distributed at the beginning of a session, and participants "work through" the contents.

—**Remote Location Training.** Books can be sent to those not able to attend headquarters training sessions.

There are several other possibilities that depend on the objectives, program or ideas of the user.

One thing for sure, even after it has been read, this book will be looked at—and thought about—again and again.

TABLE OF CONTENTS

(continued next page)

CONTENTS (Continued)

PREFACE

The fast-paced telephone techniques presented in this book are not for everyone or for every time. They are practical ideas designed for your work.

Here's proof. For a moment, remember a leisurely weekend that included a telephone conversation with someone special in your life. Recall the pleasure of hearing the other person's voice.

Isn't it true, the subject was secondary. There was no need to get to ''the point.'' Contact was the point.

When it comes to friendship and love, effectiveness is not the major concern. The call itself, the fact that contact was made and feelings exchanged, is the message. The pleasure of hearing the other person's voice is all we ask.

However, when we want to use the telephone to get someone to do something, to achieve specific results, to communicate a message effectively, these practical, proven techniques really count.

You will find the techniques in *The Telephone and Time Management* will help you get more done in less time, with fewer frustrations, and happier results. And you will enjoy the increased control over your telephone as you weave these ideas into your daily work.

Dru Scott

Dru Scott

GETTING THE MOST FROM THIS BOOK

SOME OBJECTIVES FOR YOU

You will be working with more than 50 practical, proven techniques in this book. View them as you would a buffet. Pick the ones that are most beneficial for your work responsibilities, your pressures, your priorities, and the people in your life.

Concentrate on no more than seven techniques. Selecting more than this encourages you to put them aside. Even if you only pick three or four, that's fine. When you pick the right ones for you and concentrate on putting them to work, you reap rich rewards. You will reinforce habits that will reduce stress and build your effectiveness in managing time and the telephone.

Fold the corner of this page because it's a useful place to return to as you work through the book. When you discover a technique that is good for you, write it in the spaces below. Then use the list of techniques you select to help you tackle the troublesome areas.

THE TECHNIQUES I HAVE SELECTED FOR BETTER TIME MANAGEMENT ON THE TELEPHONE

1. _____

2. _____

3. _____

4. _____

5. _____

6. _____

7. _____

SECTION I

TELEPHONE TIME STRESS

FACE UP TO TELEPHONE TIME STRESSES

"The irrelevant questions!"

"The telephone interrupts me constantly!"

"How can I ever get this person off the line without being rude?"

These sounds of stress echo throughout organizations. No one is exempt. Managers, supervisors, technicians, and front-line people are all being hit with increased demands for productivity. Pressures are greater than ever before. The pace of business is faster. More business is being conducted over the telephone than ever before.

ARE YOU GETTING SHORT-CHANGED ON THE PHONE?

When Alexander Graham Bell invented the telephone in 1876, he gave the world an invaluable communications tool. In the eyes of hundreds of thousands of workers, however, he also unleashed a tyrant. People today see the telephone as a major source of job stress—it invades their meetings, interrupts their work, cuts into their concentration, even follows them home. Worse yet, it adds to their frustrations by wasting their time. In fact, many top executives put the telephone at the head of their lists of the world's worst time-wasters.

The irony is that the telephone can be a top time-saver in today's fast-paced business environment. It can save time on travel, meetings, memo writing and letter writing. It can help us process information more rapidly, solve problems more quickly, make decisions faster.

Despite the telephone's obvious potential for saving time, however, many people get short-changed when they spend time on the phone—simply because few of us have been trained to use it effectively. It may serve almost as an extension of our bodies, something we reach for automatically and take completely for granted, and it can become a tryant when we don't know how to make it work for us rather than against us.

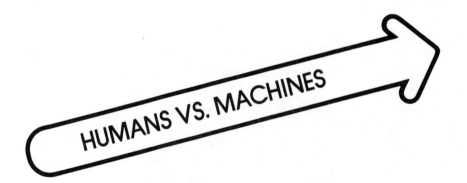

HUMANS VS. MACHINES

TELEPHONE TECHNOLOGY AND THE HUMAN FACTOR

The telephone industry is making incredible strides in developing advanced technology, and the telephone will play an ever-increasing role in our lives in the future. But this doesn't eliminate the human factor. It only underlines the importance of developing professional telephone skills.

> *When a busy law office installs the latest call director system to save time, the system is sabotaged if the telephone operator hasn't been trained to handle multiple incoming calls with courtesy and dispatch.*
>
> *If a secretary hasn't been trained to take fast, accurate and complete phone messages, the boss can waste time in frustrating callbacks.*
>
> *When an ambitious management trainee hasn't been schooled in the techniques for getting through to the people he or she wants to reach, blocks of time can be wasted on hold.*

As technology improves and the business use of the telephone increases, the demand for people who are skilled and professional in their use of the phone will also increase.

Now is a great time to explore these practical, easy-to-learn techniques for controlling your telephone time. It is your best insurance against increasing frustration, stress, and wasted time.

The first step in transforming the telephone from a time-wasting tryant into a tool for your success is to uncover your personal telephone time stresses. Listen to yourself. The quiz on the next page will enable you to recognize the causes of frustration that add stress on the phone.

ASSESS YOUR TELEPHONE STRESS LEVEL

> As you respond to each statement, be realistic. Face up to what you deal with most days. Then, in the light of your actual experience, please mark each statement:

```
N  =  Never
S  =  Seldom
F  =  Frequently
C  =  Constantly
```

1. When the phone rings, do you groan inwardly (or even out loud)?   N S F C

2. Do people call and want to socialize or engage in small talk when you have work you want to complete?   N S F C

3. Do you talk with irate people over the phone?   N S F C

4. Does your work entail telling people information over the phone that they do not like hearing?   N S F C

5. Do you find yourself clenching the receiver so tightly that your hand hurts or tingles?   N S F C

6. Are you on the telephone when you need to be spending your time on something else?   N S F C

7. Do you thumb through telephone messages several times before returning calls?   N S F C

8. Do you pick up the phone and put it down without placing the call you started to place?   N S F C

9. Do people call you with irrelevant questions?   N S F C

10. Are you personally called by people selling products or services?   N S F C

11. Do you have trouble getting access to lines or actually reaching the numbers you want?   N S F C

12. Do you search through papers for telephone messages?   N S F C

ASSESS YOUR TELEPHONE STRESS LEVEL
(Continued)

13. Do you have people waiting for you near your desk when you are on the phone?   N S F C

14. Do you call and reach a secretary or answering machine three and four times before getting through to the person you want?   N S F C

15. Do people not return your calls?   N S F C

16. Are you on hold for more than a minute?   N S F C

17. Do you have calls holding for you when you are already on the phone?   N S F C

18. Do you call from pay phones as part of your work?   N S F C

19. Do you have five or more telephone messages waiting for you to answer?   N S F C

20. Do you need to make three and four phone calls to get one answer?   N S F C

Count up the number of answers in each column:

Number of answers:

Never	_____	× 1 =	_____
Seldom	_____	× 2 =	_____
Frequently	_____	× 3 =	_____
Constantly	_____	× 4 =	_____

Total Telephone Stress Points   _____

---

45 or more stress points: The time to clean out dangerous time stress is right now.

40-44 stress points: The need to get more control over your telephone is an urgent priority.

35-39 stress points: Sharpening your telephone skills will significantly remove barriers to your productivity.

30-34 stress points: You have a good handle on managing telephone time stresses. Your improvements will all be on the plus side for you.

29 stress points: Congratulations! You have mastered the tools for managing your telephone—or you have found a job as a lighthouse keeper.

MY TELEPHONE STRESS POINTS

My highest telephone stress points (from pages 6 and 7) are:

1. _____

2. _____

3. _____

4. _____

5. _____

6. _____

7. _____

8. _____

Keep your personal telephone time stresses in mind as you read through this book. Look for the principles that relate to your specific situation. Listen for the techniques that you can tailor to your demands. Even though the potential for telephone time stress is increasing, fight back.

SECTION II

IT ALL STARTS WITH THE TONE OF YOUR VOICE

VOICE TONE SAYS IT ALL

Did you ever start the day with a telephone call that left you feeling angry or upset, and then find that all subsequent calls that day seemed to go wrong? It's the domino effect. Or have you ever worked with someone who consistently received more angry phone calls than anyone else in the office, even if he or she was transferred to new job responsibilities? The key to both problems is voice tone.

When people can't see you, your tone of voice becomes immensely important. When you are feeling frustrated or angry, that negative emotion collects in your voice. The person on the other end of the line hears it even though you may be unaware of it yourself. As a result, the person with whom you are speaking does not trust you as easily. He or she may waste your time with demands for more details and verification, will not be as cooperative or receptive to your suggestions, and may even call back to gain reassurance. Your anger and frustration will escalate, collecting in your voice and adding to your stress.

The fastest way to eliminate the problem of allowing your stress to ''show'' is to make a conscious effort to project a warm, crisp voice tone. It takes patience and practice but once achieved it will do so much to save you time, solve problems, and increase your productivity on the telephone. The warmth communicates friendliness and personal caring. The crispness adds the note of professionalism that creates the image of competence and inspires time-saving trust.

CONFESSIONS OF A MIDNIGHT OPERATOR

Sometimes the tone of voice we use over the telephone is more important than the actual message our words convey. If you don't believe it, listen to these confessions of a successful marketing executive who worked her way through college as a night telephone operator at a large metropolitan hotel.

> "I used to get bored during the slow hours late at night and early in the morning. So I invented a game to keep myself awake and alert. Keeping my voice friendly and businesslike, I'd substitute off-the-wall phrases for the usual greeting when I answered the phone.

> "I'd say things like, 'The sky is falling, may I help you?' or, 'Lemon meringue pie.' Or, 'Hopscotch and jump rope.' You know, never once during the three years I had that job was I challenged by a caller. I think it was my tone of voice that did it. As long as I sounded efficient and friendly, that's what they heard—not what I actually said."

The moral of the story, of course, is not that you should use nonsense phrases when answering the phone, but that callers listen to your voice tone before they hear your words. To gain people's cooperation faster, develop an attractive voice tone.

THE 30% SOLUTION

Have you ever called an office and heard a weak little voice answer the telephone? Chances are your immediate response was distrust of the person's competence. Here again, you are likely to waste time because you feel the need for verification.

On the other hand, you can accomplish what you want faster when you add energy to your warm tone over the telephone. A radio broadcasting manager recommends the '30% solution.' He laughingly explains, ''The transistors eat 30% of your energy. Add 30% more than your usual level and you make people want to listen to you.''

As you add more energy to your calls, you will notice that your calls get shorter. Here's why. Your energy invites others to be at their best. They are likely to think more clearly. Your tone attracts people's interest. You get their full attention.

PUT A SMILE IN YOUR VOICE

YOU CAN HEAR A SMILE

In vintage westerns, the hero used to say, "Smile when you say that, pardner," to someone venting anger. It is still good advice today—especially when talking over the phone—because people can *hear* a smile in your voice.

■ A major radio station found that they received significantly fewer complaints from listeners when their telephone talk show hosts smiled on the air.

■ Listeners calling in felt they had been cut off if the host's voice sounded the least bit impatient or unfriendly.

■ Hosts who smiled as they talked to callers drew far fewer complaints, even though they used the same language as the 'non-smilers.'

Some radio stations even place mirrors where they will reflect the host speaking on the phone. Mirrors remind everyone of the importance of putting a smile in your voice—even while racing against the clock to stay on schedule.

Use the technique yourself. It is almost impossible to sound angry when you are smiling.

THREE STRATEGIES
FOR TONING UP YOUR VOICE

Just smiling at your reflection in the mirror isn't enough if you have pent-up feelings of anger and frustration. First, release those stressful feelings. Here are three action steps that can help you do it harmlessly and quickly:

GET SOME VIGOROUS EXERCISE. Athletic activities are great for releasing negative emotions. Hitting a tennis ball with a vengeance may not improve your serve, but it will do wonders for your emotional state. A hard run, aerobic dancing, or a long, brisk walk are often alternatives.

SHOUT IT OUT. This is great for when you are driving alone in a car. Roll up the windows and shout out all the wild, hostile phrases you can think of. You may look a little strange to passing motorists, but if you release your feelings this way, you'll emerge from the car much more relaxed and better disposed to your fellow human beings.

PUNCH A PILLOW. Close the door to your bedroom, turn on the radio or TV up loud, pile several pillows on the bed, make a fist, and punch those pillows as hard and fast as you can. Yell if you want to—the radio or TV will cover the sound. Most people find this a fast, effective way to restore that friendly and businesslike tone that saves so much time on the phone

In a demanding work environment, anger is commonplace. Protect yourself and your voice from the dangers of collecting the anger day after day. If you have had a difficult day, get some exercise, shout it out, or punch a pillow. You will have a more effective voice tone when you don't let the sun go down on your anger.

IN CASE OF EMERGENCY

Emergency Cures: The One-Minute Vacation Break

Let's say you feel fine when you arrive at work, and then the first two or three calls are terrible. You realize your voice tone is beginning to have an edge of anger, and you are not about to dash home to punch some pillows. These short-cuts will get you back in shape fast. They are one-minute vacation emergency cures you can take right at your desk.

Extra oxygen—Deep breathing for 60 seconds does wonders for your voice. It calms you and helps you think more clearly because more oxygen gets into your system. If you are so upset you are having trouble concentrating, use your index finger to close your right nostril and inhale through your left nostril as you slowly count from 1 to 7. Now, close your left nostril and exhale through your right, counting slowly from 1 to 7 again. After only 60 seconds of this exercise, you will be pleased to hear your voice tone sounding relaxed again.

Relaxing moment—Another one-minute vacation involves mentally replaying a favorite, relaxing moment you enjoy. Perhaps you will choose walking along a sun-sparkled meadow with a brook, or skiing down a snow-swept hillside. Imagine the sounds of that relaxing moment. Add the tastes and smells. At the end of only 60 seconds, you will be sitting with a relaxed posture and a calm voice.

If you're feeling so pressed you don't think you can afford to give yourself a one-minute vacation, remember how much time can be wasted during a phone call when your voice tone triggers distrust in the person with whom you're talking.

CASE STUDY I

CASE STUDY

GETTING MORE COOPERATION WITH AN ATTRACTIVE VOICE TONE

You work in a busy office with a high number of incoming and outgoing calls. Many of your calls represent complaints, and the phones seem to ring all day long.

You have learned that you get better cooperation and people pay more attention when you use a warm and energetic voice tone. You have also discovered that sitting tall makes your voice sound better. You don't know for sure but suspect that the exercising you do at home helps your voice tone—and reduces your stress as well. No one taught you these things, but they seem to work for you.

You are ready for work when Sandy, a colleague from a nearby area stops by. She pulls up a chair, leans over the arm, puts an elbow on your desk and sighs.

> *"I wish I got callers like you do. They seem so cooperative. I never hear you repeating yourself to get people to understand. It makes me mad that just because I sound young, people don't pay attention to me. They should respect me. It bothers me that I need to ask people three or four times before they follow up on my requests. People should be more considerate."*
>
> *I know you recommended that I practice sitting up straight and breathing deeply. But that's just not me. It doesn't feel natural. I tried it a couple of times, but it just doesn't work. And it's not that easy.*
>
> *Does voice tone really matter that much when you are working with insensitive people? Do you have any other ideas I could try?"*

You want to help Sandy reduce her stress and get more cooperation from her callers. How would you answer these questions:

1. What are some advantages for Sandy if she develops a more attractive, warm, and energetic voice tone?

2. What specific recommendations would you make for Sandy?

3. What two things would be beneficial for Sandy to do this week?

Write your answers on the next page.

CASE STUDY—(Continued)

1. What are some advantages for Sandy if she develops a more attractive, warm, and energetic voice tone?

   _____

   _____

   _____

   _____

   _____

   _____

2. What specific recommendations would you make for Sandy?

   _____

   _____

   _____

   _____

   _____

   _____

3. What two things would be beneficial for Sandy to do this week?

   _____

   _____

SECTION III

TACKLING TELEPHONE INTERRUPTIONS

TACKLING TELEPHONE INTERRUPTIONS

You're right in the middle of a rush project with time pressures closing in minute by minute. Or you have just snapped the lock on your briefcase and are heading out the door for an important meeting. Then the phone rings. You don't want to be rude to the caller, and you do not have time to talk. What do you do?

To learn the answers, turn the page.

INTERRUPT INTERRUPTIONS

Following are three smooth steps for getting out of interruptions quickly without letting the caller feel brushed off or neglected:

1. *Say "yes" to the person.*
   Immediately use a quick phrase that lets the caller know you value him or her as a person even though you are not going to say "yes" to the call at that time. For example, here are some good possibilities:

   > *"It's good to hear your voice."*

   > *"Thank you for following up on my call."*

   > *"I'm glad you are back in touch."*

2. *Explain your situation.*
   Quickly let the person know why you are not taking the call at this time.

   > *"I'm right in the middle of a rush project just now."*

   > *"I have an important deadline staring me in the face."*

   > *"I am on my way out to an appointment."*

3. *Arrange a callback.*
   Find a time that is convenient for you both so he or she has no reason to doubt your sincerity.

   > *"What's a good time for me to call you back tomorrow?"*

   > *"Would it be convenient for me to call you back between 2:00 and 4:00 this afternoon?"*

   > *"Can I call you tomorrow before noon?"*

The moment you hang up the phone, reach for your calendar. Jot a quick note to call the person back at the promised time. When you write notes on callbacks in your calendar, you free yourself from having to waste time reminding yourself to call. You are able to focus fully on what you need to do right now. You are more creative and energetic about tackling the work at hand.

PUT A CLOCK ON PERSONAL CALLS

The most complicated interruptions are often the personal calls. Because the conversation is close to home, it is easy to let a personal call run longer than you expect. With the spiraling costs of telephone service and people's time, everyone is paying more attention to these costly interruptions.

THE 8-MINUTE PERSONAL CALL CHECK

If you spend more than 8 minutes a day on personal phone calls at work, it may be a signal that you're having a problem handling these interruptions. To find out just how much of your time they are eating up at work, clock the personal calls you make and receive for the next three days. If they total more than 8 minutes a day, consider the benefits of keeping them within that limit:

> You'll reduce the necessity of needing to work late to make up time lost in personal calls.

> You'll build cooperation with co-workers, who are much more willing to help you when you need it if they know you've been sticking to your job.

> You'll free yourself to handle occasional personal emergency calls without guilt or pressure.

Here are examples of gracious and effective phrases that incorporate the three steps to interrupt interruptions described on page 18.

> *"I want to hear all the details of your vacation. What is the best time to call you at home this evening so we can have a long talk?"*

> *"It's good to hear your voice. It is difficult for me to talk right now. Let's set a date for lunch this week so we can chat without interruptions."*

> *"Honey, I'm glad you had a good day at school. I need to get back to my work. Go ahead and do your homework and we'll talk all about your day over pizza tonight."*

> *"I'm glad you called about your new job, and I want to hear all about it. I am under a lot of pressure right now. When is the best time to call you back, after 5:00 p.m.?"*

Friends and family who are in the habit of calling you at work to chat will soon get the message that the best time to talk to you about personal matters is *not* during working hours. And at the same time, they will be reassured by your friendly style.

HELP YOUR CALLERS COME TO THE POINT

HOW TO GET CALLERS TO COME TO THE POINT FAST

You have been interrupted by the phone. On top of that, some of your callers seem to take forever to get to the point of their call. It may be fun to replay last Sunday's football game or to discuss vacation plans when you have time to spare, but when you don't, here are two phrases that courteously invite callers to get to the point of their call fast:

"What can I do for you?"

"How can I assist you?"

You help people get what they want when you lead them directly with a fast-start question.

TWO PREREQUISITES FOR THIS POST GRADUATE TECHNIQUE

To prevent coming across abruptly, you can use these two prerequisites as you ask the question:

1. *Physically smile.* (Yes, this makes an amazing difference.)

2. *Lift your voice at the end of the question.* Even with the right wording and the right voice tone, if you drop your voice at the end of the question, you may come across too brusquely.

Practice it for yourself. Use a tape recorder or ask a friend to listen to you. Say each phrase—once smiling and lifting your voice at the end, and once again dropping your voice at the end. The second time will sound colder.

Using one of these two phrases lets your callers know that you are ready to be of service and want to assist them. You save everyone's time and avoid hurting anyone's feelings. And you eliminate one more potential source of stress from your telephone time.

BRIDGE BACK TO YOUR POINT

Often it is easier to get people to come to the point than it is to keep them focused on it. Some callers are forever straying off the subject to ask irrelevant questions or waste time in idle chit-chat. You can sidestep these digressions and get the conversation back on course courteously by using the Bridge Back Technique.

Pick out a word or feeling from the other person's comments, mention it, and then come back to your point. Here are some examples:

DIGRESSION:	BRIDGE BACK:
"I'm so tired of storms. I am tempted to get on a plane and join you in the sunshine."	*"Speaking of storms, there will be one in this office if I don't finish this report for you today."*
"Boy, wasn't that an exciting game last night?"	*"It really was. And I'm even more excited about our new product line."*
"Your logo looks great. How did you ever come up with that?"	*"I'm glad you like it. I'll put a brochure in the mail to you today that gives the background on our logo. That way we can keep moving ahead on our agenda for the meeting Wednesday."*

WRAP IT UP WITHOUT BEING RUDE

Has this happened to you? You have gotten the caller to the point and have kept the conversation on course. You have finished the real business of the call but your caller keeps talking. You don't want to sound rude, but you do need to end the conversation and get back to other work.

Here are the techniques that get you around this roadblock:

1. *Talk in the past tense.* You can say, ''It has been good talking to you,'' or, ''This has been a very productive call,'' or, ''I'm glad we had a chance to talk.''

2. *Close with points and promises.* Summarize the call. This is particularly effective when you want to conclude a call that covered a number of points. You can say, ''To summarize what we've discussed,'' or, ''Let me go over my understanding of the points we've agreed upon.'' You not only end the call, you avoid misunderstandings that can generate time-wasting callbacks.

3. *Spell out follow-up action:* ''I will follow-up on your suggestion and get back to you before noon tomorrow.'' ''I appreciate your checking into that question for me and look forward to hearing from you before Friday.''

4. *Say ''Thank you.''* This is a universal signal that the conversation has come to an end. Here are some suggestions: ''Thank you for calling. Is there anything else we need to cover before we say 'goodbye'?'', or ''Thank you for calling. Is there anything else we need to discuss before we say 'goodbye'?''

Years ago, the etiquette books dictated that the caller had responsibility for ending the call. That rule no longer holds true. In today's busy world, both the person calling and the person called have the responsibility for using time wisely. Even if you are the person called, it's correct to take the initiative in closing a call gracefully. Remember, you are saving the caller's time as well as your own.

Telephone interruptions are inevitable in the course of a busy day, and you can tackle them successfully when you use these techniques:

1. Say "yes" to the person.
2. Explain your situation.
3. Arrange a callback.
4. Use key phrases to get callers to come to the point fast.
5. Use the Bridge Back Technique to keep the conversation on course.
6. Wrap it up without being rude.

SECTION IV

GETTING THROUGH TO PEOPLE

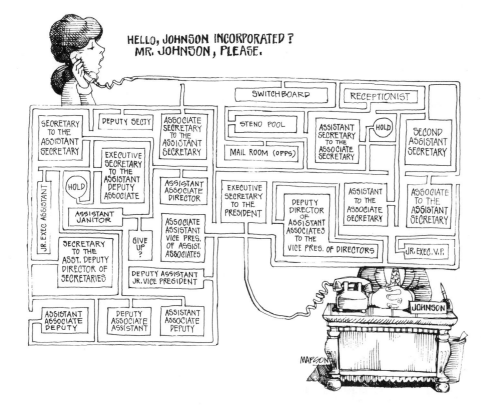

REACHING THE PERSON YOU ARE CALLING

Sometimes getting through to people you want to reach
resembles laying siege to a medieval castle. There seem to be
formidable barriers in the way. Perserverance helps, and the
quickest way to success is to plan your strategies and practice
to make them perfect.

FIVE STRATEGIES FOR REACHING YOUR TARGET

When you want to get through to a busy person who doesn't know you, it's particularly important to be skilled in these time-saving strategies.

1. *Use a confident tone.* When you use a confident tone of voice and communicate personal warmth, you'll discover that people are much more likely to help you.

2. *Use confident terminology.* Delete all downers from your telephone vocabulary.

   The most common ones include:

   > *"He's probably not in, but . . ."*
   >
   > *"She may not want to talk to me, but . . ."*
   >
   > *"I've been trying to reach her for days, but she's always out!"*

   Confident terminology includes expressing appreciation of the person handling the call:

   > *"Thank you for taking my messages. I appreciate your help in getting Mr. Smith and me together."*
   >
   > *"I'm going to be out of my office a great deal. What would be the most convenient time for me to call Ms. Jones?"*
   >
   > *"I hear your other line ringing; would you like me to hold for a moment?"*

3. *Explain why you are calling, and highlight benefits to the person called.* The key is to focus on what you want to *give* not what you want to *get.*

   > *"I know. Ms. Brown's schedule is very full. What is the best way for us to get this information to her about how to reduce purchasing costs?"*
   >
   > *"Mr. Smith mentioned that he's studying new ways to increase productivity. I've developed an approach that fits the special needs of your office. When is the best time for me to call to give him the highlights?"*

FIVE STRATEGIES
FOR REACHING YOUR TARGET (Continued)

4. *Be creative in your timing.* If you are having trouble getting through to someone despite repeated calls, phone before the start of the normal business day. Many busy individuals get an early start and can be reached between 7:00 and 8:00 a.m.—before the onslaught of the regular business day's demands.

5. *Open the way with a letter.* Some people make repeated phone calls, but don't have the perservance to sit down and write a letter when they can't get through. A letter often works when telephone calls alone won't. It helps you organize your thoughts, gives you an opportunity to headline the benefits you offer, and demonstrates that you are serious about wanting to communicate with the person. It can also serve as leverage when you make your next call. You have a springboard for getting the conversation off to a fast start when you can ask, "Did you receive my letter of April 18th?"

USE THE FIVE W'S AND AN H

How frustrating is it to hang up the telephone after an important call and barely have the receiver out of your hand only to remember a key point you forgot to mention. Or how many times have you been talking with someone and let your mind wander as you lined up your own thoughts? Your listening stopped as you regrouped. There is a fast way to prevent these frustrations.

Borrow an idea from professional journalists. Prepare yourself by writing a headline. Make sure you have thought through:

- ☑ **WHY**
- ☑ **WHAT**
- ☑ **WHEN**
- ☑ **WHO**
- ☑ **WHERE**
- ☑ **HOW**

You give yourself an added advantage when you focus on the "why" and "what" first. You may discover that a telephone call is not the best way to accomplish what you want.

Before you pick up the phone to make an important call, actually note the headline that focuses on the purpose of the call. With other calls, all you may need to do is add a few key words to jog your memory on the points and questions you want to cover. Then check off the points and questions as you talk.

Headlining your call saves time in a number of ways. It helps you organize your thoughts and present them more effectively. It provides you with a checklist of points to be covered, thereby reducing the need for additional calls on the same subject. It also provides you with all the information if you should need to leave a message. When the callback occurs, both you and the other person are better prepared to talk.

Perhaps most important, headlining your call and listing the points you want to discuss enables you to get to the point quickly and to keep the conversation on course.

DON'T GROW OLD ON HOLD

You do everyone a favor when you state the purpose of your call as soon as you've given your first and last name. When people know what you want to discuss, they can communicate more accurately if they need to place you on hold to check with the party you are calling.

The marketing vice president of a major corporation joked at a national meeting, ''Our sales figures would have been higher, but our sales reps kept being put on hold.'' It got a big laugh from the audience, but it's no joke when you are feeling trapped on hold. The minutes tick by, punctuated only by a repeated, ''Hold please''—followed by long stretches of silence or by canned music that's supposed to make prisoners of the hold button feel less abandoned by the world.

The next time you find yourself being asked three or four times to, ''Hold please,'' be assertive. As soon as the other person comes back on the line, say immediately, ''Please don't put me on hold again!'' You gain at least a few seconds of highly focused listening time from the somewhat startled operator. That's your opportunity to leave a message, find out when is the best time to call back, or perhaps even persuade that person to put you through right away. When you do get through to leave word, have your ammunition ready—a complete message.

REDUCE CALLBACK CONFUSION

| LEAVE COMPLETE MESSAGES |

For all-around time-wasting, the incomplete message heads the list. You will save yourself—and the people you call—time, confusion, and stress by polishing your skill in leaving complete messages quickly and smoothly. Here's how:

1. *Give your first and last name, and the name of your organization.* (Don't wait for the other person to pry this information out of you. Avoid awkward moments while he or she tries to guess who is calling.) It only takes one or two seconds.

2. *Give your telephone number automatically.* Maybe the person you are calling talks with you frequently and already has your number; however, few of us memorize all the phone numbers we call often. Don't assume your number is in his or her automatic dialer. Save the person you are calling the time it takes to look up your number. It is courteous to give your number without being asked.

3. *The pause pays off.* Avoid a confusing string on run-together numbers. Pause after each number group so the person taking the message has time to hear it and write it down accurately. Be sure to include the area code if you are calling long distance. For example, rather than saying, ''4157512234,'' say, ''Area code four-one-five (pause), seven-five-one, (pause), two-two-three-four.''

You will both avoid the wasted time of having to repeat numbers, and the greater time-waste of getting the number wrong.

4. *Say why you want the person to call you back.* Have you ever returned a call only to discover that you needed to do some research before giving your caller the requested information? When you leave a complete message, you avoid that pitfall. When people know *why* you want them to call, they will be better prepared to assist you. For example:

''Please ask her to call me about the arrangements for the monthly meeting.''

''Please ask him to call me to discuss the Rockford contract.''

SECTION V

HIGH-TECH TELEPHONE ETIQUETTE

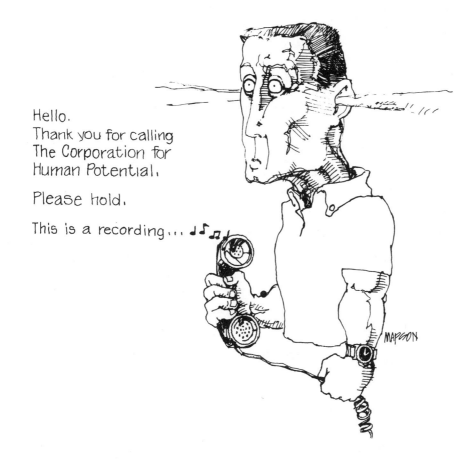

Hello.
Thank you for calling
The Corporation for
Human Potential.

Please hold.

This is a recording...

NEW TELEPHONE ETIQUETTE

Today's demanding work pace and dazzling telephone equipment raise questions about traditional telephone etiquette. The old rules are out. What was correct and worked in the past is showing the worn edges of obsolescence.

The purpose of this section is to:

■ Focus on the frustations today's changes are bringing.

■ Pull together practical ways of coping.

■ Apply some penetrating techniques for preventing these irritations.

SMOOTH YOUR TRANSFERS

Do the frustrations aired in the following letter sound familiar?

Dear Author:

Help! This afternoon was the last straw! I needed to track down one piece of information, and I was transferred five times in the process. I felt brushed off and kicked around.

People have no idea how badly it comes across when they tell you, ''You have the wrong number.'' Or, before you can get two words out, they issue the ultimatum, ''I have to transfer you.''—Click. No one listens to what I need!

I go home and kick the cocker spaniel and complain to my family. Why don't people learn how to use the telephone?

(Signed)
Transfer Trauma

Dear Trauma:

Spare your spaniel, and demand your rights! Some transfers are inevitable. The irritations are not. We have a right to a reason before being shuttled on to a new number. We have a right to a request rather than an arbitrary command.

(Signed)
Author

GIVE REASON AND THEN REQUEST

When you explain the reason and then express your request, you prevent frustration. You take the sting out of the necessary evil of transferring.

It's true; people are much more patient and cooperative when they know the reason why. This needed courtesy only takes a few seconds.

Listen to these examples and see how they smooth the irritation out of transfers:

Reason:
''Nelson Smith has the information you are calling about. You can reach him on extension 1234.''

Then Request:
''May I transfer you, or may I take your name and number and ask him to call you?''

Reason:
''Our information center will tell you which office can answer your questions.''

Then Request:
''May I transfer you to them on extension 2345?''

SMOOTH YOUR TRANSFERS (Continued)

HEAD OFF THE STRAY INTERRUPTION

You can use Reason then Request to keep people who need to call someone else away from you. You save your time and the time of others when you ward off the potential misdirected call.

Rather than:
"You should be talking with Jim Smith on my staff instead of interrupting me with these questions."

Give Reason then Request:
"Jim Smith now has all the latest specifics on your question, and he can give you the most up-to-date answers. May I ask him to call you, or is it better to transfer you to him?"

(After listening to the answer, add:)
"In case you would like to make a note, his number is 234-5678."

(To express how much you value the caller, close with:)
"If something unusual comes up and you don't get everything you want, call me back."

Because your situation has differences and special considerations, tailor the format to your style. Develop your own Reason then Request responses.

Dear Author:

"It's not that easy. I used to help poor misdirected souls, but no more! Once they got my name and number, they called me for everything. All I was doing was herding the lost through our company maze. I couldn't get my own job done.

(Signed)
No More Good Guy

Dear Good Guy:

Self-protection is in order. When you are assisting callers, make it easy for them not to call you back.

(Signed)
Author

POSITIVE SELF-PROTECTION

| POSITIVE SELF-PROTECTION |

Experiment with these self-protection possibilities.

"For future use, you might want to make note of this number I'm transferring you to."

"Since you have been transferred several times already, I will call the purchasing office for you and give them your message. To save you time in the future, here is the number you can call directly."

In addition, make a few fast notes. This draining problem needs to be solved. Get the facts about the type of questions and the number of calls involved. Make sure this information gets into the hands of the persons who can take preventive action. Your organization may need more informative telephone directories or streamlined information services. Design systems that get everyone off to a good start.

FOUR SECONDS TO A FAST START

How many times have you muddled into a confusing call only to have the situation cleared up with, *"You mean, this isn't the Reproduction Office?"* The caller has given you two paragraphs of information because he or she didn't recognize in what office you were.

Prevent this problem. Answer your phone with the name of your department. If you have an operator or receptionist who initially receives calls, leave off the name of the company. Otherwise, include the organization name. If your company has a long name, use a shortened version.

The final portion of that four-second fast start is to give your first and last name. Even if people do not remember it, saying your full name communicates that a trustworthy human being is on the line.

PROPER USE OF NAMES

USE FIRST AND LAST NAME TO BUILD CONFIDENCE

Imagine you are lying in a hospital bed. Your doctor has told you that a specialist will talk with you about a crucial operation you must have. In walks a man in a white coat. He smiles and says, *"I'm Nick, your brain surgeon."* How would you feel? Would that first-name-only introduction do much to build your confidence?

That's an extreme example. However, it illustrates an important point about answering the telephone in a professional situation. If someone answers a call with, *"Credit Department. Ms. Jones Speaking,"* it comes across as condescending and too formal. On the other hand, a breezy, *"Credit Department. Sandy Speaking,"* doesn't convey a professional image. Time will be wasted in building confidence in the caller. Giving only your first name may also create time-wasting confusion if there is more than one Sandy in your organization.

The best way to answer the telephone in a work situation is to give the name of your organization and both your first and last name. It is a courtesy to the caller because it immediately communicates business-like competence. Names are not just a formality. They are important.

"BUT WE'RE REALLY INFORMAL AROUND HERE"

This comment expresses good intentions that often miss the target. Not everyone wants to be called by his or her first name. Give people a choice. Start off by addressing them with a more respectful title. A "Mr. Williams" or "Ms. Williams" never hurts. Then the caller has the choice of saying, "Please call me Jim," or, "Please call me Martha."

If your caller is angry, use the more respectful address. It lets the other person know you are taking the situation seriously. Experiment with respectful address. You will discover some pleasing pluses.

Names are an example of how only a word or two can make a big difference. You will gain people's cooperation much more quickly. Focus on a few key words that people appreciate listening to, and you will save more time and solve more problems when answering the phone.

USE KEY WORDS TO SOLVE PROBLEMS

KEY WORDS SOLVE MULTIPLE PROBLEMS

As you listen to these problem responses, you will think of laughable examples you have heard yourself.

> *"She went to the doctor because she has been having problems with her digestive tract."*
>   (This is being too helpful.)

> *At 10:00 a.m.: "She hasn't come in yet."*
>   (What the person does not say is that she might have worked until 10:00 p.m. the night before.)

> *At 1:00 p.m.: "He is still out to lunch."*
>   (And you suspect the next comment might be, "And he has been out to lunch for the last year."

Even though these situations differ, one generic response handles them all smoothly and professionally:

> *"He (or she) is out of the office right now. May I take a message, or is there some way I can assist you?"*

I used to say "desk" rather than "office," until a savvy person brought me up-to-date with, "It may only be a desk to you, but it's *my* office."

A man in a high tech start-up firm claimed the best response is, "She is away from her performance module right now." Stick with "office." Some traditions are worth it.

THE ART OF TAKING MESSAGES

In a survey of 200 people, a surprising complaint cropped up. The purpose of the survey was to assess why some employees developed poor reputations and suffered from blocks in their careers. The list included predictable items such as "lack of motivation," "poor attitude" and "unwillingness to learn". Surprisingly the list also included, "not taking complete telephone messages". The indictment fell across the board. With lean staffing (especially in support functions) people who never took telephone messages a few years ago, now find themselves taking messages for others. Make sure when taking messages, you do not neglect the Six Essential Steps (shown on the facing page).

SIX ESSENTIAL STEPS TO TAKING MESSAGES

| THE ESSENTIAL SIX |

How many times have you wasted time following up on an incomplete message? Maybe the message just says, "Call Charlie." No phone number, no last name, no clue as to whether it's Charlie your barber, or Charlie your friend from Chicago, or Charlie the lawyer you are working with on that construction problem.

You may make three calls before getting the right Charlie. Even if there is only one Charlie in your life, you still need to spend time looking up his number. And when you reach him, you may learn that he wants to talk about something you need to dig out of the files. So you hang up, find the information, then call Charlie back a second time.

When you take a message, it saves everyone's time (and temper) if you follow these few easy rules:

1. *Get the full name;* if you don't understand it clearly or it isn't a familar name, ask the caller to spell it for you. Use wording like this: "I want to make sure your message is accurate. Will you spell your name?" Delete the condescending, "Does he (or she) know you?"

2. *Ask for the name of the organization.* It's a good reminder and a way of double-checking if there is a mistake with the number.

3. *Get the full telephone number, including the area code if its long distance.* If the caller says, "She has it," you can say politely, "I know she can get back to you even faster if I jot your number down with your message."

4. If the caller doesn't volunteer any specific message, it will save time on the callback if you ask, *"Is there any information you would like to leave* that may be helpful to Ms. Jones when she calls you back?"

5. *Say, "Thank you," and tell the caller that you will give the person the message*—it is reassuring. Avoid saying, "I'll *have* her call you." It sounds bossy. "I'll ask her to call you," is more professional.

6. *Note the time and date the message was taken, and add your initials* in case there are any questions.

SCREENING CALLS

Even though it may take a few seconds longer at first, you will easily save others 5 to 15 minutes in looking up numbers or making wasted callbacks when you take complete messages.

"NOT AVAILABLE" IS O.K.

"He is in a meeting," "She is in a conference," and, "He is busy right now," have been so misused they are best tossed into the inactive file.

In today's pressure-filled business climate, it is correct to say, "He (or she) is not available right now." There are times when work at hand takes precedence over the phone. "Not available" is correct form today.

SCREENING WITH STYLE

Irritation is no surprise when an individual calls, is asked for his or her name, and then is told that the person being called has left for the day. It may be true; however, it sounds like a brush-off.

If the person being called is not available, state that first. Then ask for the caller's name. This technique is not only more courteous, it builds trust and saves time.

"Who's calling?," gets on the irritation list also. Somehow it sounds rude and preemptory, even when it is not meant to be. A more thoughtful expression is, "May I tell him (or her) who is calling?" (If someone comes back with a joking, "Yes," then ask, "What is your name please?")

Since screening is a fact of life, it deserves to be handled in a streamlined and considerate manner.

SCREENING CALLS (Continued)

STREAMLINE YOUR SCREENING STRATEGY

Today, people at all levels are adopting the strategy of being:

> Totally Available
> With Blocks of Not-Available Time

This system has major advantages:

1. You can have blocks of time to concentrate and double your productivity.

2. The system is fair without sounding condescending. The person answering your phone is not put in the bind of intimating to callers, ''I-can-put-you-through-if-you-are-important-enough.''

3. When you have scheduled Available Time, your callers know in advance the best times to reach you.

There are many ways to tailor this strategy to different situations.

A tax accountant is able to concentrate during the busy season and still provide clients with timely service by asking his assistant to tell callers,

> *''He will be available between 11:00 and 12:00, and again between 4:00 and 5:00. May I take a message, or would you prefer to call back then?''*

Three customer service representatives in a large corporation did some brainstorming and came up with this creative solution. On a rotating basis, two take on the extra calls and give the third person one afternoon a week of Not-Available Time. This oasis away from the telephone provides an opportunity to wrap up complicated work that defies completion in ten-minute segments.

An engineer carves out a block of Not-Available Time by turning on her telephone recorder the first two hours in the morning and the first two hours in the afternoon.

If you are confronted with work that demands concentration, then experiment. Discover a system that will serve you. Being Totally Available with some blocks of Not-Available Time will help you. After you get the system going, the people you work with will respect your improved productivity. They will also respect your directness and consideration.

WHEN CALLS ARE ON HOLD

USE THE ONE-MINUTE HOLD RULE

Sixty seconds is a long time to dangle on hold. As an experiment, set a timer and experience how long a 60-second wait feels. Chances are you will feel edgy and irritated long before one minute is up.

Someone calls you, and you need to get additional information. If you suspect your research will take longer than a minute, don't subject your caller to that irritating period on hold. Offer to call back. Even though you will have the added expense of the return call, this technique takes the pressure off you. You can concentrate on finding the information, and you give people the right answer the first time.

When you are talking on one line, and another call comes in, here's what to do:

1. Put the first person on hold.

2. Answer the second line with a phrase like this, *"Smith and Company. This is Sandy Clark. I'm assisting someone on another line right now. May I have your name, organization, and number, and I will call you back."*

3. Immediately jot down that name, number, and organization.

4. Return promptly to the first call. Don't waste time in excessive apologies. A warm, quick *"Thank you for waiting,"* is more courteous and it gives the conversation an upbeat continuation.

Using the hold button efficiently saves time, and it calls for specific techniques. When you are putting someone on hold, state the reason first, then make the request. For example:

"I have another call coming in. Will you please hold for a moment?"

"I need to get some information. Will you please hold?"

"Mr. Jones has the information you want. Will you please hold while I check with him?"

Take time to wait for a reply after asking, *"Will you please hold?"* It only takes a few seconds, and it is more courteous to the caller. If there are unusually rushed times when you do not want to wait for an answer, simply say, *"Thank you for holding."*

CALLBACK STRATEGIES

THE CALLBACK CRISIS

Dear Author:

Help! As I picked up the telephone receiver this afternoon and heard the angry voice, I groaned to myself, "How could I have forgotten to return this man's call? I promised I would get right back to him this morning." Then ten other emergencies broke out, and I didn't call him back. And I thought about that call a dozen times during the morning too.

The telephone is beating me into a corner, and I'm losing the fight.

(Signed)
Callback Crunched

Dear Crunched:

The fight isn't over. You can win the fight against callbacks. Arm yourself with the Call-Back-Before Technique.

(Signed)
Author

CALL BACK BEFORE 10:00, 12:00, 2:00 OR 4:00

When you say you will call someone back, be specific about the time. Instead of saying, *"I'll call back in half an hour,"* or *"I'll call back tomorrow,"* use the Call-Back-Before 10:00-12:00-2:00-4:00 Technique. It will save you time and help you concentrate.

Here's how it works. Draw two crossing lines on a section of your desk calendar each work day. Mark the quarters 10:00, 12:00, 2:00 and 4:00.

Next, when you tell someone you will call back say, *"I'll call back before 10:00"* (or whatever time is best for the situation). Then immediately write the callback commitment in the appropriate time block.

You will save time two ways. You free your mind from the distracting necessity of reminding yourself to call back "in half an hour." You group your callbacks so you can make them sequentially.

Here's an extra time-saving tip. Begin making your callbacks at least 30 minutes before the 10:00-12:00-2:00-4:00 deadlines. You will be under less pressure, and that will help you think more clearly and creatively while telephoning.

Today	
10:00 a.m.	12:00 noon
2:00 p.m.	4:00 p.m.

CALLBACK STRATEGIES (Continued)

"IS THIS A CONVENIENT TIME TO TALK?"

When you do call back, you can increase your popularity and gain full attention. After you quickly introduce yourself and the purpose of your call, ask, *"Is this a good time to talk?,"* or, *"Do you have a few minutes to talk right now?"*

Your question shows your respect for the other person's time. It gives him or her a graceful opening to tell you immediately if your call has come at a difficult time.

KEEP THE MOMENTUM GOING

You have your callback system and wording practiced and working. Prevent breaks in that momentum by listening for a dangerous three-letter word that cuts into the flow of thinking. The word is "but." It breaks the movement of your conversation.

Replace "but" with "and." "And" connects and keeps people with you. It adds a plus to your message that makes the hearer more receptive to what you are saying.

Check for yourself. Haven't you followed someone's line of thought only to hear the word "but," and you subsequently lost the idea that came before that disruptive little word?

Listen to the difference between these examples:

Rather than:	Replace with:
"I can get that information for you, but I have to call you back with it.	*"I can get that information for you, and I will call you back with it."*
"I would to talk, but my other phone is ringing. Can I call you back before noon?"	*"I would like to talk, and my other phone is ringing. May I call you back before noon?"*
"I will be happy to work on that project, but I can't get to it before tomorrow morning."	*"I will be happy to work on that project, and I will get to it tomorrow morning."*

CALL BACK STRATEGIES (Continued)

| REPLACE "HELP" WITH "ASSIST" |

"Help" can trigger a defensive reaction. Some will equate being helped with being helpless. It can sound as if a person is not competent to handle his or her own affairs.

"Assist," on the other hand, suggests your desire to satisfy one of their independent, enrichment wants.

Replace "help" with "assist" and you will gain people's cooperation and confidence.

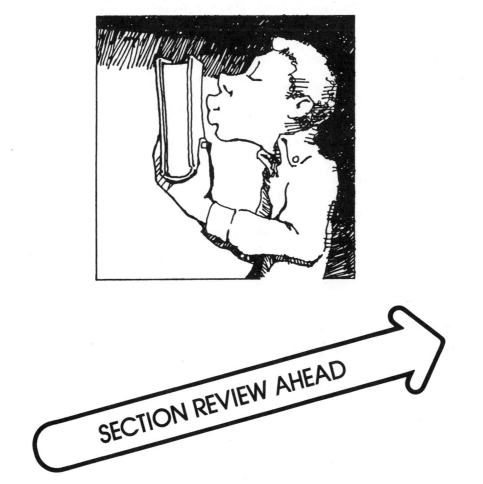

SECTION REVIEW AHEAD

REVIEW

Up-to-date telephone etiquette does assist us in working with today's dynamic stream of events. That stream touches every aspect of our lives and challenges us to re-think basic ways of working with people.

The practical guidelines in this section open the door to productive telephone time for you and the people with whom you work. Following is a check list of the main points which should help you improve your telephone etiquette:

☐ Give the Reason then the Request, and you take the sting out of transferring.

☐ Indulge in positive self-protection.

☐ Head off the stray interruption by helping people call the right person next time.

☐ Build confidence and give yourself a fast start by answering with your first and last name.

☐ Polish your skill in using a few key words to solve multiple problems.

☐ Re-discover the vanishing art of taking time-saving messages.

☐ Build your productivity with creative blocks of Not-Available Time.

☐ Use the One-Minute Hold Rule.

☐ Free yourself with the Call-Back-Before 10:00, 12:00, 2:00 or 4:00 Technique.

☐ Smooth out challenging situations with "and" and "assist."

SECTION VI

USE FRIENDLY WORDS

FAST AND FRIENDLY WORDING

"But I don't want to be rude because people get irritated and won't cooperate."

This concern is voiced by many thoughtful people. They need to get their work done in less time, and they are not willing to do so at the price of running roughshod over others.

There is a solution. Many people have developed sound shortcuts. These people get the results they want, and at the same time they get cooperation. They have discovered the secret of using Fast and Friendly Wording.

When you put the expressions in this chapter into your daily calls, you benefit in two big ways:

1. You have fewer delaying, uncooperative people over the phone.

2. You feel more energetic because you are communicating in the most efficient way. No wasted motion or energy.

Use the Fast and Friendly Wording and you will have fewer irritated and uncooperative people. It's guaranteed.

CLEAN UP THE "DIRTY" WORD LIST

How do you feel when you hear these dirty words? To get a specific feeling for the negative impact, please put a check mark on the continuum after each item.

The Dirty Word List
When you hear each expression, how do you feel?

	Irritated or Hesitant	Cooperative and Energetic
"You have to..."	•————————————————•
"You should have..."	•————————————————•
"I'll try"	•————————————————•
"You made a mistake"	•————————————————•
"Your complaint"	•————————————————•
"You can't..."	•————————————————•
"We can't..."	•————————————————•
"As soon as possible"	•————————————————•
"I'm just..."	•————————————————•
"There's nothing I can do"	•————————————————•
"Why didn't you..."	•————————————————•

As you consider the following examples, pick the ones that have the most value for you in reducing your telephone demands.

"You have to..."   *"Will you..."*

These first three words account for more lost business and angry people than any other three words in the English language. How do you feel when someone commands you with, *"You have to..."*? We instinctively react negatively to these three words and as a consequence we are less likely to cooperate with someone who says, *"You have to."* The second two words take no longer to say, and are much more likely to get the fast action you want.

MORE FAST & FRIENDLY WORDING

Rather than:	Replace with:
"You have to call extension 25."	*"Will you call extension 25?"*
"You have to submit that in writing."	*"Will you let us have your request in writing?"*
"You have to have that information in by April 15th."	*"Will you let us have the information by April 15th? That's the final deadline."*

"Will you . . ." also replaces the next dirty phrase.

"You should have . . ."   *"Will you . . ."*

The first phrase focuses on the mistake or problem. The caller feels defensive and wants to justify his or her actions. The second phrase focuses on the solution and the steps that need to be taken to achieve the objective.

Rather than:	Replace with:
"You sent your request to the wrong department. You should have sent it to me."	*"Will you resubmit the request and mail it directly to me? I'll make sure it is taken care of."*
"You should have talked to Mr. Blume about that. Now he won't be back in town until next Friday."	*"Will you bring it up at next Friday's meeting when Mr. Blume is certain to be there?"*
"You should have gone to the front door. This door is kept locked."	*"I'm sorry. That door is always locked. Will you come around to the front door?"*

MORE FAST & FRIENDLY WORDING
(Continued)

Not only does the Fast and Friendly replacement build cooperation, it is faster. You will save time with the next example too.

"I'll try..."   *"I will..."*

When you cannot guarantee a specific result, delete the word "try" and substitute "I will," with specific steps you intend to take.

Rather than:	Replace with:
"I'll try to get that information for you."	*"I will check our production department and our shipping records, and I will call you back."*
"I'll try to have your computer run ready by noon tomorrow."	*"I will give your job a rush priority. Since you need it by noon, and since we have several rush jobs to complete, I'll call you first thing tomorrow to let you know the status."*

The second option avoids making promises you cannot guarantee, and it avoids the brush-off sound of "try." You also let the caller know that you are taking specific actions on his or her behalf. This helps the caller be more understanding when you do not phone back immediately with the results.

If you find that you do not have the information at the promised time, call anyway. A quick call retains your credibility. For example, *"I don't have all the information I need in order to give you the status report. That data will be ready at 9:00. May I call you then?"*

The next Fast and Friendly substitute reveals another good place to use, *"Will you please..."*

MORE FAST & FRIENDLY WORDING
(Continued)

"You made a mistake"   *"Will you please..."*

"Will you please...?" avoids the defensive reaction. It moves straight to solving the problem.

Rather than:	Replace with:
"You made a mistake in calling us. We don't have that information."	*"Will you call Product Information? They can answer your questions."*
"That's the wrong coding. You made a mistake."	*"Will you check the new coding guide and include those codes on your order?"*

"Your complaint"   *"Your question"*

The word "complaint" sets up a defensive reaction that the word "question" does not. You will find "question" an appreciated substitution.

Rather than:	Replace with:
"Your complaint was referred to my office."	*"Your question was referred to my office."*

"Your problem"   *"This situation"*

When there is a possibility of someone's feeling defensive, substitute the word "situation" for "problem." People will be more cooperative.

Rather than:	Replace with:
"What can we do to solve your problem?"	*"What can we do to solve this situation?"*
"Here's what we can do to solve your problem."	*"Here's what we can do to solve this situation."*

MORE FAST & FRIENDLY WORDING
(Continued)

"You can't..."
"We can't..."   *"You can..."*

Nobody likes to be told they can't do something. Tell them what they *can do* instead.

Rather than:	Replace with:
"You can't come in on Saturday; we're closed."	*"You can come in Monday through Friday between 9:00 a.m. and 5:00 p.m."*
"You can't talk to Mr. Jones until tomorrow."	*"You can reach Mr. Jones tomorrow after 9:00 a.m."*
"We can't get the report completed today."	*"You can have the report the first thing tomorrow."*
"We can't give you Monday or Friday off. It's too busy then."	*"You can have Tuesday off. The workload is too heavy Monday and Friday."*

When you tell people what they can do instead of what they can't, you say "no" in a professional manner that saves time and encourages cooperation.

"I will call back   *"I will call back*
as soon as possible."   *before _____ o'clock."*

"As soon as possible" can mean within the next two minutes in one situation and by the next fiscal year in another. You might say, *"I'll get that data for you as soon as possible,"* and know that the research will take you at least two hours. To prevent your caller from waiting by the telephone with bated breath, give a specific time you will phone back.

Rather than:	Replace with:
"I will get back to you as soon as possible."	*"I'll call you back before 10:00 a.m. today."*

Giving a specific time is not only a courtesy to your caller, it gives your mind the ease of remembering, *"10:00 a.m."* rather than a sliding *"as soon as possible."* You also prevent frustrating interruptions. And if 10:00 a.m. is not acceptable to your caller, you discover that immediately rather than suspecting and dreading it.

MORE FAST & FRIENDLY WORDING
(Continued)

Here is additional proof. You have two projects dropped on your desk. One is labeled, ''Complete before May 1st''; the other says, ''Complete as soon as possible.'' Most of us will complete the project with the specific deadline *before* we do the ''as soon as possible.''

''There's nothing   ''I will _____ ''
I can do.''   (list specific action)

Though the options open to you may be limited, the person calling you can erupt into a rage at hearing, ''There's nothing I can do.''

Rather than:	Replace with:
''There's nothing I can do.''	*''I'm going to put this on my calendar for next Wednesday, and I will check on your request again, and I will call you at that time.''*

Even with limited options, there is always something you can do.

''Why didn't   ''Will you...''
you...''

Lead directly into solving the situation by asking for the action that will straighten things out. *''Why didn't you...''* sounds too much like a scolding to be practical for use on the job.

Rather than:	Replace with:
''Why didn't you call the Accounting Department about this situation?''	*''Will you please call the Accounting Department about this situation?''*

Another great way to get things rolling in the right direction is to ask this question: *''What can we do right now to solve the situation?''* Smile when you say it, and be prepared to repeat it again. When people are anticipating an attack, they may not listen very well.

MORE FAST & FRIENDLY WORDING
(Continued)

Dirty words are costly. They trigger irritation and hesitation. They drain your energy.

Dirty words are common. You can hear them every other phone call. On the radio, they crop up in every other song. It is easy to let them slip into your language. Fight back!

Scan the summary of dirty words. Circle two or three that have special impact on your work.

Dirty Words:	Fast and Friendly Substitutes:
"You have to..."	"Will you please..."
"You should have..."	"Will you please..."
"I'll try..."	"I will..."
"You made a mistake"	"Will you please..."
"Your complaint"	"Your question"
"Your problem"	"This situation"
"You can't..."	"You can..."
"We can't...	"You can..."
"As soon as possible"	"Before _____ o'clock"
"I'm just..."	"I am..."
"There's nothing I can do"	"I will _____ (list actions)"
"Why didn't you..."	"Will you please..."

Give yourself an extra edge. Put the Fast and Friendly substitutes you picked on a 3″ × 5″ card near your telephone.

You will enjoy how much faster people cooperate with you when you sprinkle Fast and Friendly wording into your phone conversations.

SECTION VII

SET THE STAGE FOR YOUR SUCCESS

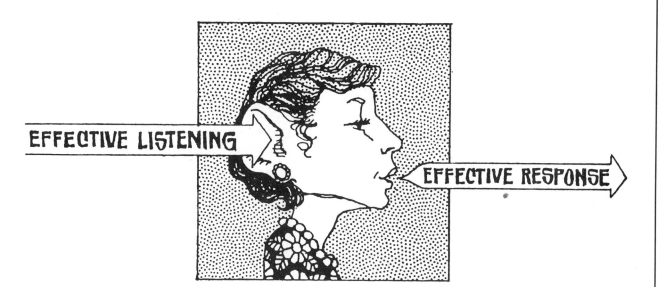

EFFECTIVE LISTENING

EFFECTIVE RESPONSE

WHY ORGANIZATION IS ESSENTIAL

Getting your job done through the telephone demands creativity and energy on its own. When your physical environment is not working to help you, it doubles the drain on you. The purpose of this chapter is to assist you in putting your physical environment to work for you.

First, let's focus on the irritating problem of scrambling and searching to find messages and documents. Turning the telephone into a tool rather than a tyrant means being able to find what you want, when you want it, without wasting time searching.

However, turning the telephone into a tool does not necessarily mean your desk must look a certain way.

ORGANIZE YOURSELF FOR SUCCESS

| A MESSY DESK IS THE SIGN OF A MESSY DESK |

People across the country confess they feel guilty about the way their desks look. How a desk looks is not the issue.

Some people have desks that look like Atilla the Hun worked there, and still find what they need. Other people have work areas with the look of a surgical operating room, and they also find what they need. There is no correlation. Workability—not apprearance—comes first.

The question is, does your desk—your office—work for you? Take this quick quiz to see how your physical setting measures up.

1. Can you find any needed information within three minutes? ☐ Yes ☐ No

2. In your absence, can your colleagues or co-workers find needed information within three minutes? ☐ Yes ☐ No

3. Does your desk invite you to tackle your work and get the job done? ☐ Yes ☐ No

If you answered "yes" to all three of these questions, it does not matter what your desk looks like. It is working for you. (The exception to this conclusion is the organization where having an orderly-looking desk helps your reputation within the company. In that situation, it is worthwhile to keep your desk shipshape anyway.)

ORGANIZE YOURSELF FOR SUCCESS
(Continued)

CLUTTER vs. CLUTTER PROBLEMS

The Find-Anything-Within-3-Minutes Test decides whether you have clutter, or clutter problems. If you checked three "yes's," skip ahead to the section on The Wonderful World of Telephone Technology.

The rest of us can eliminate searching time with the use of the following simple and fast tools. The first of these is an easy habit you are probably already enjoying to some extent.

MAKE TIME-SAVING NOTES A HABIT

A few pertinent notes on important calls will save you all kinds of time and frustration later. They underscore your memory and remind you of commitments and deadlines.

FOUR QUICK THOUGHTS ON NOTE-TAKING

1. *Make your notes during the call*—not after. The phone has a way of ringing again right after you hung up, or someone drops in. Notes delayed are notes not made.

2. *Make note-taking a habit.* People tell me it's too time-consuming to jot down a note. I don't agree. I absolutely guarantee that the habit of note-taking will save you far more time than it takes. I've researched this claim in over a dozen major corporations. People who make a few simple, concise notes while they talk are more productive.

3. *Date your notes.* This step really saves time and confusion, and offers you quick recall.

4. And here is the last quick tip. *Keep all your telephone notes in one place* unless there is a specific file or spot for the information. Keep your notes in a notebook or a binder or wherever you choose, but always use the *same* place. The note that doesn't clearly have a special place is the problem to find.

USE A TELEPHONE JOURNAL

You will find that keeping your notes in a telephone journal will eliminate 90% of searching time. Your journal doesn't have to be complicated. Use a three-ring binder with dividers. Here are some section divisions you can use or adapt to your situation.

> *Frequently Called Numbers*—To start with, be certain your journal has a section for numbers you call frequently. This is a real time-saver since you call 20% of your numbers 80% of the time.
>
> *Frequent Questions and Where to Get the Answers*
>
> *Telephone Notes*—You can subdivide this section by the month, or by some other convenient chronological unit.

A practical format for telephone notes within your journal is to set up individual columns for *Date, Time,* and *Person.* Include a column marked *"I"* for incoming calls, and another marked *"O"* for outgoing calls, so you can put a check mark in the appropriate column. Finally, the most important column is headed *Points and Promises* where you write brief notes on the points covered and the promises made for follow-up by parties to the call.

Today's demand for increasing productivity strips away the luxury of confirmation letters in many situations. Much more business is conducted over the telephone today, and your telephone journal is a fast and accurate record. You clear away time-wasting questions by having the references, handy, and can say with assurance, "We agreed to these three points in our conversation of August 15th..."

Experiment and design a journal that suits your style.

Do you put everything in your telephone journal? There is no need for a note on, "Send up a tuna fish on rye." With some things, I will never need to follow-up or record.

Time-consuming? Overkill? Here is another promise. A journal like this will save you ten minutes for every minute you spend on it. And you will be in control. It is a logical companion to keep near your telephone.

GIVE YOUR TELEPHONE SOME SPACE

GIVE YOUR TELEPHONE SOME SPACE

Provide yourself with an easy-to-use telephone environment. A special place helps you concentrate.

If possible, put your telephone on a desk return or credenza, or at least isolate it from your main work area as best you can. This way you will need to turn to use the phone, and that helps you concentrate on the call and reduces the chance of split-attention mistakes.

Leave your telephone's most important accessories next to it at all times—a pencil and pad. Better yet, keep your own telephone journal right there for immediate note-taking.

Remember how many times you have called an office and had someone tell you, "Wait a minute while I get a pencil and a piece of paper." This lapse is even more startling in light of today's sophisticated equipment.

THE WONDERFUL WORLD OF TELEPHONE TECHNOLOGY

Check out all the new systems and innovations in the wonderful world of telephone technology. Focus on the equipment and features that will help *you* solve *your* particular telephone time problems.

Do you want to save the time to dialing those frequently called numbers? Consider a speed dialer or memory phone that will automatically dial popular numbers for you at the touch of a button.

Do busy or un-answered phones trouble you? Get a persistent dialer that will automatically redial the last number called—for hours if necessary—until the line is answered, leaving you free to use your time more fruitfully.

Are you interrupted too frequently by the telephone when you are facing a deadline? Have a simple on/off switch installed on your phone.

TELEPHONE TECHNOLOGY (Continued)

TELEPHONE TECHNOLOGY (Continued)

Are you expecting an important call, and you don't want to waste valuable telephone time by keeping your line clear until it comes? A call-waiting feature will warn you when there's an incoming call even while you are on the line with someone else.

Do you talk too long? Mount a miniature clock/stopwatch on your phone. It will save you time and money.

Do you need to keep your hands free while you talk—perhaps to locate a file or move about your office? Get a speaker phone that allows you hands-free conversation.

You might even consider a speaker phone attached to an automatic dialer. With this combination of features you won't have to pick up the phone until the other person is actually on the line.

For truly hands-free conversation, how about a voice-activated phone? You can dial and talk without even pushing a button.

You might also consider telephones that allow you to wander: a cordless phone; a battery-operated headset; one of the new and less expensive car phones. All are time-savers.

Conference calls are great time-savers for when you don't want to wander. They save travel, time and money, and are often more productive than in-person meetings.

When you're not available to take your own calls, and don't want to miss any messages, a voice messaging system may be your answer. Your callers' messages are recorded completely and stored the first time they phone. No more guessing games about why a person is trying to reach you. When you are again available, you dial in for your messages and hear them in the caller's own voice.

The point is, find anything and everything that will help you make your telephone communications easier or faster. One word of caution. Don't go overboard on the new telephone technology. Don't let it become an end in itself.

There is no doubt about it. New telephone innovations are numerous and ingenious and everchanging. Match these new features with your needs and you will use your time more effectively.

TELEPHONE ANSWERING MACHINES

BEAT THE MACHINE

As time demands increase, more and more businesses are using telephone recorders for messages. Here are three tips for recorded messages:

1. *Dont' be cute.* It wastes everyone's time.

2. *Leave and invite concise, complete messages. "Hi, George, This is Tom. Call me. You have the number."* This message is concise, but not very complete if George knows more than one Tom, or has lost Tom's number. Here is a much more effective message: *"This is Tom Evans of Eviteck Controls. Will you call me Tuesday morning before 10:00 about the Potter proposal? My number is 456-7890."*

3. *Don't be intimidated by the beep.* Be prepared instead. It is amazing how many articulate people "er" and "ah" and "well" when they deal with recorders. The solution is preparation. If a recorder answers when you phone, use as your message the headline you prepared before placing the call.

If you are recording a greeting to leave on your own answering machine, use something like this:

> *"Thanks for calling. Please leave your name, organization, and number. So I'll be prepared when I return your call, will you also tell me how I can assist you?"*

If the same people call you frequently, change your message every two or three weeks. Even a slight change will give some welcomed variety.

In spite of all the telephone technology available, you may still be wrestling with major time stresses.

FIND THE REAL VILLAIN

If you still feel that the telephone is eating up too much of your valuable time, face up to it and learn where that time is going.

Don't panic. You don't need to keep a multi-columned, multi-colored, multi-complicated telephone log. Instead, be especially aware for five days of how you use the telephone.

Ask yourself these five questions about each call you make or receive:

1. **With whom did you talk?**

2. **Who initiated the call?**

3. **What was covered?**

4. **What was achieved?**

5. **How long did you talk?**

Making a few notes can lead to some very valuable insights. Typically, a small group of people is wasting your time on the telephone. Often, you are a villain yourself—inviting or placing too many time-wasting calls or interrupting yourself. Or maybe incomplete messages are the culprit. Or personal calls. Or poor screening.

The critical point is to analyze how your telephone habits or other factors waste your time. Then you can acquire the skills, or the equipment, or the discipline to correct the situation.

MAKE THE SYSTEM WORK FOR YOU

Your telephone is only a tool; it can't do the best job for you until you develop professional skill in using it.

Today there are dozens of capabilities built into the various telecommunications systems on the market. You may be missing out on valuable services that your telephone system offers—features that can help you save time and reduce stress.

Take the time to discover what your system can do for you. Talk to your communications manager or to a representative of the company that installed your system. Go to your training director. Get the information you need to tailor the system you have to your job requirements and personal style of working.

You deserve a physical environment that works for you. Concentrate on what helps you turn your telephone into a productive tool.

Skip feeling guilty about a messy desk if you can find anything within three minutes.

If you are cleaning up a real clutter problem, design and use a telephone journal that assists you in keeping on top of things.

Make time-saving note-taking a habit.

Put the spotlight on your telephone by giving it some special physical space.

Make the answering machine a tool for your efficiency by using practical and polished messages.

If telephone time stresses are still battering you, use the 5-question check-up to uncover the real villain.

GETTING THE MOST FROM YOUR TELEPHONE AND YOUR TIME

Rather than reaching out to embrace dozens of ideas that you want to use more frequently, take hold of three or four techniques from this book. Concentrate on developing your skill with this select group.

Use your choice techniques again and again until they feel natural. Practice them until you develop the smooth grace of an athlete. Enjoy your heightened skills.

Your skills rest on these twin realities:

The best time-saver of all is to listen.

and

The best courtesy of all is to lead.

Your skills flourish with a regular reminder. Whenever you touch a telephone, remind yourself of the basics. Picture these words:

The challenges are varied. The techniques many. The basics few.

SECTION VIII

WORKSHEETS FOR GROUP USE: SUMMARY & REVIEW

WORKSHEETS

The next few pages contain worksheets which were designed to help practice several of the concepts presented in this book. We hope you will enjoy using them as you apply techniques you have learned for better TIME MANAGEMENT AND THE TELEPHONE.

INTERVIEW #1—THE TELEPHONE: TOOL OR TYRANT

To help you get to know people and to reinforce productive ideas, talk with another person using these questions as a guide for your discussion.

Please introduce yourself to someone nearby, and ask each other the following questions.

At the end of the interview time, please be prepared to summarize what you learned or relearned.

INTERVIEW #1:   WITH: _____
(name)

1. What are the most difficult telephone time management situations you handle?

2. What are some telephone time management problems or opportunities you have *in common* with the person are you interviewing?

3. What are some telephone time management problems or opportunities you have that are *different* from those of the person you are interviewing?

4. What do you do to reduce the stress that may come from heavy telephone demands? For example, using streamlined wording that is fast and courteous.

5. How do you reward yourself when you handle a tough situation skillfully?

INTERVIEW #2—THE TELEPHONE: TOOL OR TYRANT

Now please introduce yourself to another person, and ask each other the following questions.

At the end of the interview time, please be prepared to summarize what you learned or relearned.

INTERVIEW #2:   WITH: _____
                                    (name)

1. Assume someone calls you and talks on and on before getting to the point of the call. Why might a person be so long-winded?

2. When a caller takes a long time to get to the point, specifically what can you do?

3. What are courteous and effective ways of wrapping up a call with a talkative person who keeps on talking after finishing the purpose of the call? Will you please be specific.

4. What can you say to a co-worker who is not doing the best possible job of handling the telephone, who asks you for help, and who then claims, ''I know that already!''?

INTERVIEW #3—THE TELEPHONE: TOOL OR TYRANT

To help you get to know people and to reinforce productive ideas, please find a third person, and ask each other the following questions.

Please be prepared to summarize what you learned or relearned at the end of the interview time.

INTERVIEW #3:　　　WITH: _____
　　　　　　　　　　　　　　　　　　(name)

1. How do you feel when you get telephone interruptions?

2. When do you get the most telephone interruptions?

   Time of day: _____

   Day of week: _____

   Time of month: _____

   Other: _____

   _____

3. What specific techniques can you use to handle both telephone interruptions and paperwork responsibilities? For example, you might write your daily objectives on your calendar so that you can get back on track more quickly after an interruption.

4. What are practical ways you can prevent some of your interruptions?

TURN YOUR TELEPHONE INTO A TIME MANAGEMENT TOOL

Will you mark each question either:	SA for Strongly Agree
	A for Agree
	NO for No Opinion
	D for Disagree
	SD for Strongly Disagree

1. The person placing the call is always the one who ends the call.

   SA   A   NO   D   SD

2. It is a good idea to include these words when you transfer a call: "Let me give you the number in case you get cut off."

   SA   A   NO   D   SD

3. It is a waste of time to make notes about the point of the call before you make it.

   SA   A   NO   D   SD

4. Writing a headline about what you want to achieve in a call helps you be more respectful of the other person's time.

   SA   A   NO   D   SD

5. The best idea is to make your follow-up notes after you make the phone call. That way you can concentrate during the call.

   SA   A   NO   D   SD

6. If the caller wants to spend a long time on chitchat before you get to the purpose of the call, there's nothing you can do.

   SA   A   NO   D   SD

7. If someone wanders from the point of the conversation, you can tactfully mention a word or feeling from the other person's comments and bridge back to the point.

   SA   A   NO   D   SD

WHEN YOU HAVE FINISHED, FIND SOMEONE WHO IS ALSO FINISHED AND DISCUSS YOUR ANSWERS.

PRACTICE AND USE FAST & FRIENDLY LANGUAGE®

Will you mark each question either:	SA	for	Strongly Agree
	A	for	Agree
	NO	for	No Opinion
	D	for	Disagree
	SD	for	Strongly Disagree

1. You save yourself time when you learn guide language for recurring situations.　　SA　A　NO　D　SD

2. People would rather hear something spontaneous than something that is effective.　　SA　A　NO　D　SD

3. If you have heard Fast & Friendly Language® once or twice, you will automatically know it.　　SA　A　NO　D　SD

4. If you know Fast & Friendly Language®, you will automatically use it.　　SA　A　NO　D　SD

5. If something isn't easy, it is not worth doing.　　SA　A　NO　D　SD

6. If you use some of the proven techniques and you are not satisfied with the results, conclude that your situation is different and they don't apply.　　SA　A　NO　D　SD

7. The way to learn a new skill is similar to becoming a fine athlete. It takes practice and repetition.　　SA　A　NO　D　SD

WHEN YOU HAVE FINISHED, FIND SOMEONE WHO IS ALSO FINISHED AND DISCUSS YOUR ANSWERS.

DOUBLE-CHECK YOUR SKILLS— THE TELEPHONE: TOOL OR TYRANT

Based on the book, **The Telephone and Time Management** by Dru Scott, Ph.D. and the film, **The Telephone: Tool or Tyrant** produced by the Cally Curtis Company of Hollywood.

RATHER THAN
ORDINARY LANGUAGE:

REPLACE WITH
FAST & FRIENDLY LANGUAGE® :

1. *"He's out to lunch."*

   _____
   _____
   _____
   _____
   _____
   _____

2. *"Services Department. Sandy."*

   _____
   _____
   _____
   _____
   _____

3. *"You have to call the Accounting Department on extension 1234."*

   _____
   _____
   _____
   _____
   _____

4. *"I'll call you back in 15 minutes."*

   _____
   _____
   _____
   _____
   _____

DOUBLE-CHECK YOUR SKILLS—THE TELEPHONE: TOOL OR TYRANT (Continued)

RATHER THAN
ORDINARY LANGUAGE:

REPLACE WITH
FAST & FRIENDLY LANGUAGE® :

5. *"Who's calling?"*

_____
_____
_____
_____
_____
_____

6. *"Please call Charlie."*

"Charlie _____
with _____
at (_ _ _) _ _ _ - _ _ _ _
about _____
_____
_ _ _."

7. *"Does she know your number?"*

_____
_____
_____
_____
_____
_____

8. *"You have to call extension 25."*

_____
_____
_____

9. *"You have to submit that request in writing."*

_____
_____
_____
_____
_____

70

RATHER THAN
ORDINARY LANGUAGE:

REPLACE WITH
FAST & FRIENDLY LANGUAGE® :

10. *"Let me give you the
number in case you get
cut off."*

_____
_____
_____
_____
_____
_____

11. *"You sent your request to
the wrong department.
You should have sent it
to me."*

_____
_____
_____
_____
_____
_____

12. *"Your complaint was
referred to my office."*

_____
_____
_____
_____
_____
_____

13. *"You made a mistake in
calling us. We don't
have that information."*

_____
_____
_____
_____
_____

14. *"I will get back to you as
soon as possible."*

_____
_____
_____
_____

RATHER THAN
ORDINARY LANGUAGE:

REPLACE WITH
FAST & FRIENDLY LANGUAGE® :

15. *"You can't come in on
Saturday. We're closed."*

_____
_____
_____
_____
_____
_____

16. *"We can't get the report
completed today."*

_____
_____
_____
_____
_____
_____

17. *"I'll try to get that
information for you."*

_____
_____
_____
_____
_____
_____

18. *"There's nothing I can
do."*

_____
_____
_____
_____
_____
_____

NOTES

FOR OTHER FIFTY-MINUTE SELF-STUDY BOOKS
SEE THE BACK OF THIS BOOK.

FOR OTHER FIFTY-MINUTE SELF-STUDY BOOKS
SEE THE BACK OF THIS BOOK.

NOTES

FOR OTHER FIFTY-MINUTE SELF-STUDY BOOKS
SEE THE BACK OF THIS BOOK.

FOR OTHER FIFTY-MINUTE SELF-STUDY BOOKS
SEE THE BACK OF THIS BOOK.

NOTES

FOR OTHER FIFTY-MINUTE SELF-STUDY BOOKS
SEE THE BACK OF THIS BOOK.

NOTES

FOR OTHER FIFTY-MINUTE SELF-STUDY BOOKS
SEE THE BACK OF THIS BOOK.

NOTES

ABOUT THE FIFTY-MINUTE SERIES

We hope you enjoyed this book and found it valuable. If so, we have good news for you. This title is part of the best selling *FIFTY-MINUTE Series* of books. All *Series* books are similar in size and format, and identical in price. Several are supported with training videos. These are identified by the symbol **v** next to the title.

Since the first *FIFTY-MINUTE* book appeared in 1986, millions of copies have been sold worldwide. Each book was developed with the reader in mind. The result is a concise, high quality module written in a positive, readable self-study format.

FIFTY-MINUTE Books and Videos are available from your distributor. A free current catalog is available on request from Crisp Publications, Inc., 1200 Hamilton Court, Menlo Park, CA 94025.

Following is a complete list of *FIFTY-MINUTE Series* Books and Videos organized by general subject area.

Management Training (continued):

Personal Improvement:

Human Resources & Wellness:

Human Resources & Wellness (continued):

Communications & Creativity:

Customer Service/Sales Training:

Small Business & Financial Planning:

Adult Literacy & Learning:

Career/Retirement & Life Planning: